TRUE
Healing

Colin Urquhart

Kingdom Faith Resources Ltd.
Roffey Place, Old Crawley Road,
HORSHAM West Sussex, RH12 4RU
Tel: 01293 851543 Fax: 01293 854610
E-mail: resources@kingdomfaith.com
www.kingdomfaith.com

First published in Great Britain in March 2003 by Kingdom Faith
Kingdom Faith Trust is a registered charity (no.278746)

Unless otherwise stated, Scripture taken from the
HOLY BIBLE, NEW INTERNATIONAL VERSION.
Copyright © 1973, 1978, 1984 by International Bible Society.
Used by permission of Hodder and Stoughton Limited.

ISBN 1-900409-46-1

Acknowledgements

I praise the Lord Jesus for the wonderful privilege of seeing so many people healed through His grace and power. I trust this book will lead to many others receiving their healing from Him.

I am thankful to all who have assisted in the preparation of this book, especially Mary, David and Cliss.

I also want to honour all who have shared with me in faith during these past 40 years of ministry, especially my wife Caroline and my children, Claire, Clive and Andrea, all of whom are used in various ways to bring God's healing power into the lives of others.

Colin Urquhart

CONTENTS

GOD THE HEALER — 7

THE FOUNDATION OF FAITH — 11

FAITH TO BE HEALED — 17

JESUS HEALS TODAY: THROUGH HIS WORD — 25

SPEAKING TO THE MOUNTAINS — 33

SPEAKING THE WORD — 45

RECEIVING MINISTRY — 51

LAYING ON OF HANDS — 57

'HEALERS' — 63

HOLY COMMUNION — 65

POSTSCRIPT — 69

FURTHER READING — 71

1

GOD THE HEALER

Scripture makes it clear that God is by nature the One who heals. When we ask Him to heal we are not asking Him to do something against His nature but what is in direct line with His will.

God cannot change; *"Jesus Christ is the same yesterday and today and forever" (Hebrews 13: 8).* Yet long before He became man, God revealed to His people that it is His nature to heal.

> *I am the LORD, who heals you. (Exodus 15: 26)*

This is one of God's covenant names - the ways in which He revealed Himself to His people to show them His character, and what He wanted to do for them as His own people. Moses said:

> *Who is like you - majestic in holiness, awesome in glory,*
> *working wonders? (Exodus 15: 11)*

The awesome, holy, mighty God is the One who heals us. If He is the almighty Creator of the Universe, He certainly has the ability to mend what He has made! It is very important to understand that it is His nature to heal, for God always acts according to His nature and never does anything contrary to His nature. When He sent His Son into the world, Jesus said:

The thief comes only to steal and kill and destroy; I have come that they may have life, and have it to the full. (John 10: 10)

Because He is the Creator, God wants to impart life. Jesus demonstrated this, not only by the great number of people He healed, but also in giving eternal life to all who believed in Him. The thief is the devil. Just as God wants to impart life, so the devil wants to cause death. He wants to steal people's health and well-being. He desires to destroy whatever is good.

Jesus, on the other hand, came to reveal God's purpose in saving, healing and restoring His people. In the New Testament the Greek word translated "save" also means "heal." The Lord's saving purposes are His healing purposes. His desire to heal is, therefore, part of His total plan of salvation.

This means that He not only is able to heal, but wants to heal. Many who do not question that God is Almighty, who believe that nothing is impossible for Him, nevertheless question whether He wants to heal them. They ask the question: "Even if He is able to heal me, does He want to? Is this His purpose for me?"

JESUS WILLS TO HEAL

At the very beginning of His ministry on earth Jesus gives us the answer to such questions. The first healing miracle recorded by Matthew is that of the leper who came to Jesus with conditional faith: *"Lord, if you are willing, you can make me clean." (Matthew 8:*

2) Jesus simply removed the condition; He took away the word 'if'!

> *Jesus reached out his hand and touched the man.*
> *"I am willing," he said. "Be clean!" Immediately he was*
> *cured of his leprosy. (Matthew 8: 3)*

This is very significant. Jesus not only reveals that it is His will to heal, but as soon as the condition was removed, as soon as there were no doubts, the healing took place.

Jesus emphasised that faith was essential when praying: *"If you believe, you will receive whatever you ask for in prayer." (Matthew 21: 22)* **It is impossible to trust God to give you anything unless you first believe it is His will to give you what you ask in prayer.** He is not likely to give you anything against His will!

IT IS IMPOSSIBLE TO TRUST GOD TO GIVE YOU ANYTHING UNLESS YOU FIRST BELIEVE IT IS HIS WILL TO GIVE YOU WHAT YOU ASK IN PRAYER.

Therefore before you pray with faith, you need to know the Lord's will in the matter. Concerning healing, then, you need to be sure of His will. How can this be possible? Many hope that He will heal them, but they are far from certain that the healing will definitely take place. Their doubts are encouraged by previous experience, or because they have heard of others who have prayed with apparent faith, but have not received their healing.

I say 'apparent faith', for we shall see that often people think that they are in a position of faith for their healing when truly they are not. So we need true faith to receive true healing.

2

THE FOUNDATION OF FAITH

Faith must have a foundation; it is not a matter of believing our own thoughts, ideas and opinions. For a Christian the foundation of faith is the revelation of truth found in the Bible, and particularly all that God has already accomplished through His Son, Jesus Christ.

When we pray for God to heal, the substance of our faith lies in what God has already done, especially in the cross. A key scripture is found in the prophecy of Isaiah, written some 700 years before the crucifixion. The prophet is given, not only an accurate description of what happened to Jesus, but also its significance:

> *Surely he took up our infirmities and carried our sorrows,*
> *yet we considered him stricken by God, smitten by him, and afflicted.*
> *But he was pierced for our transgressions, he was crushed for our*
> *iniquities; the punishment that brought us peace was upon him,*
> *and by his wounds we are healed. (Isaiah 53: 4-5)*

There are a number of extremely important truths we need to grasp from these verses if we are to understand, not only that God wants to heal, but that He has already done everything necessary to make it possible to receive that healing.

- **The Hebrew words translated 'infirmities' and 'sorrows' include physical as well as emotional and spiritual needs.**

- **Jesus was deliberately sent to the cross by His Father,** a remarkable act of sacrificial love for us.

- **God wanted His Son to be 'stricken' and 'afflicted' so that we could be set free from everything that afflicts us. The work of the cross meets every need we could ever have, of the spirit, soul or body.** He was pierced to make it possible for us to be forgiven.

- **He completely identified with the very worst of conditions men could ever experience.** Jesus was 'crushed'. He knew, as He hung on the cross, what it meant to feel totally crushed by the events taking place, by what was happening to Him.

- **Jesus suffered on our behalf the punishment we deserve for our sins, so that now we can have peace with God.** This 'peace' is extremely important in God's healing purposes. Sickness is 'dis-ease'. Even much physical sickness is caused through stress and a lack of peace. The medical profession tells us that at least 70% of physical sickness is psychosomatic: it begins in the mind. To have peace of mind is, therefore, a very significant part of God's healing purposes.

- **By His wounds we are healed. To God this healing involves a complete restoration to health in spirit, soul and body.** Note that this healing has happened. All that is needed for our healing today has already been accomplished through all that Jesus did on the cross! If we look at the whole of this prophecy of the cross *(Isaiah 52: 13 - 53: 12)* we see many phrases that demonstrate **Jesus' complete identification with us in our needs so that we can now be completely identified with Him in overcoming those needs!**

"His appearance was so disfigured" - He identified with those who are disfigured.

"He had no beauty or majesty to attract us to him" - as He hung on the cross. He identified with all who feel they have no beauty, either physically or in the way they think about themselves.

"He was despised and rejected by men" - Many today suffer the negative effects of rejection and feel despised. They also despise those who rejected them. Jesus identified with all this to set men free from all the effects of rejection.

"A man of sorrows" - He identified completely with those whose lives seem to be a constant tale of sorrows, one negative experience after another. All this sorrow He took upon Himself to set people free and give them a life of joy instead!

"He was pierced for our transgressions, he was crushed for our iniquities" - All the guilt of our sins was laid on Him, so that we might be set completely free from this great burden of our sins.

"By his wounds we are healed" - He was wounded physically, as well as rejected, so that all our physical wounds might be healed.

"He was oppressed and afflicted" - Even those who feel oppressed, as if they are hemmed in or living under a great weight that is pressing down upon them, can know that Jesus suffered what they experience, so they may be set free!

"By oppression and judgment he was taken away" - Those who have suffered through being judged unfairly have One who died on their behalf, so that they can be liberated from all the negative emotions that arise out of a sense of being dealt with unjustly.

"The suffering of the soul" - Your soul consists of your mind, emotions and will. So Jesus suffered in His soul, so that you can be healed of any need that afflicts your mind or emotions.

So we see the complete identification of Jesus with our human condition and need. But how does this help us? How can a man dying on a cross nearly two thousand years ago effect our complete healing and deliverance today? We need to understand the answers to these questions to enable us to believe in all Jesus has accomplished for us on the cross.

When God became man in Jesus, He came *"full of grace and truth" (John 1: 14)*. He came with the truth of the gospel, the good news. He came to give, for God's grace is His willingness to give everything to those who deserve nothing!

There is no need of good news without bad news. The bad news was the reason why it was necessary for God to send His Son into the world. All had sinned and fallen away from the glory that God intended for mankind. Man deserved to be punished for his sin against God. He deserved condemnation and judgment: eternal separation from God.

The sickness and death that pervaded society were the consequences of the sinful state into which mankind had fallen through disobedience to God. However, in His great love for us, the heavenly Father wanted to restore us to unity with Himself. He wanted to provide forgiveness of our sins so that we could be put right with God and be enabled to live holy lives in obedience to His will. **He wanted to free us from every negative that the devil has been able to instigate because of man's fallen state: all oppression, sickness and bondage.**

HE WANTED TO FREE US FROM EVERY NEGATIVE

God could not shrug His divine shoulders and say that our sin did not matter. It had caused the separation from God and made us vulnerable to evil, including the ability to become sick. This does not mean that a person's sickness is necessarily the direct consequence of his or her sin, but that the fallen, sinful state of mankind had enabled sickness, violence and many other evils to afflict society.

To remedy the situation God needed a Man who would live in perfection; who would obey Him and do all He asked of Him. Jesus therefore had to live a sinless life and resist every temptation and attack of the devil. He had to live in the world sharing our weakness, be tempted in every way as we are, and yet withstand all sin, sickness and evil. This He did.

Then He had to make His life an offering to the Father on behalf of all who have sinned, have been oppressed, sick or crushed by the events of life. Because men deserved death for their sinful state, Jesus suffered the death they deserved, to enable them to receive life instead: His life, eternal life, God's life, life in all its fullness.

With this life came forgiveness, healing and deliverance from every need.

At the outset of His ministry Jesus said what was needed to receive this life, the life of God's heavenly Kingdom.

"The time has come," he said, "The Kingdom of God is near. Repent and believe the good news!" (Mark 1: 15)

The good news could now replace the bad news. **God had provided the necessary remedy for sin, sickness, oppression and rejection and every other need, in the crucifixion of His Son.** The Sinless One offered His life for sinners; the Perfect for the imperfect; the Healthy for the sick!

Now God's judgment on sin had been satisfied, His life could flow freely into the lives of all who believed in His Son, Jesus, as both Saviour and Lord, as the Good Shepherd who laid down His life for the sheep, as the Healer and Provider of His people.

So we have reached a significant point. God has the power to heal, for He is the Creator of the Universe! He has the desire to heal, as Jesus made clear to the leper. And on the cross He has already accomplished everything necessary for us to be healed in spirit, soul and body.

Now all that remains is to see how we can receive the healing He has made possible. There is no single way to receive, but many. However, implicit in all these ways is the faith that expects Jesus to release into our lives NOW what He accomplished THEN - on the cross.

3

FAITH TO BE HEALED

During His ministry on earth Jesus honoured the faith that others placed in Him. Immediately after the healing of the leper, Matthew records Jesus' encounter with the Roman Centurion whose servant lay sick. Jesus offered to come to the soldier's home to heal him, to which the centurion replied:

> *Lord, I do not deserve to have you come under my roof.*
> *But just say the word, and my servant will be healed.*
> *(Matthew 8: 8)*

Even Jesus marvelled at this man's faith. He had not encountered such faith among His own people, not even among His chosen disciples; and here was a Gentile soldier expressing faith that Jesus only need to give the order and his servant would be healed. As a soldier the man understood authority and could see that Jesus acted with an authority that could only be given to Him by God. The centurion continued:

> *"For I myself am a man under authority, with soldiers*
> *under me. I tell this one, 'Go,' and he goes; and that one, 'Come,'*
> *and he comes. I say to my servant, 'Do this,' and does it." When*
> *Jesus heard this he was astounded. (Matthew 8: 9-10)*

EVERY DEMONIC POWER AND SICKNESS WAS DEFEATED BY JESUS ON THE CROSS

As an officer, the centurion expected immediate obedience from those under his authority. Yet he knew he only had this authority because it was given to him by those superior to him, under whose authority he acted. He could see that Jesus could only exercise such authority because He was under authority - a truth that apparently no one realised. **Only operating under God's authority could Jesus simply speak words and people were healed.** Jesus said to the centurion:

> *"Go! It will be done just as you believed it would." And his servant was healed at that very hour. (Matthew 8: 13)*

Such things were happening regularly. Later that same day, *"many who were demon-possessed were brought to him, and he drove out the spirits with a word and healed all the sick." (Matthew 8: 16)*

Matthew makes it clear that those healings were taking place in fulfilment of the prophecy from Isaiah, demonstrating that he clearly understood **every demonic power and sickness was defeated by Jesus on the cross:**

> *This was to fulfil what was spoken through the prophet Isaiah: "He took up our infirmities and carried our diseases." (Matthew 8: 17)*

How can this be? For the cross has not yet taken place! Jesus is still very much alive as He ministers to all those people in their needs. Matthew understood that part of the Messiah's call was to overcome the devil and all sickness. What He did during the few years of His ministry in one nation, was made available to all people of all nations at all times through the cross. This means that today Jesus can heal with a Word. He only has to speak, to issue the order and a person can immediately be healed!

When He sent the Twelve out to preach the gospel, He gave them authority to issue such orders:

> *He called his twelve disciples to him and gave them*
> *authority to drive out evil spirits and to heal every disease*
> *and sickness. (Matthew 10: 1)*

What Jesus Himself did, He gave authority to the disciples to do in His name, on His behalf. The same authority is given to believers today!

However, we need to understand that Jesus never acted independently of His Father in heaven. He says that, even though He is the Word of God that came to live among us, He spoke no words of His own, only those given Him by His Father. He did nothing of Himself; He initiated nothing. He did only what He saw His Father doing. The Father was acting through His Son in the works Jesus was performing.

In other words, Jesus was acting in the name of His Father, on His behalf. He did not have to use a formula; "I heal you in the name of my Father." He never said any such thing. But to act in the name of the Father is to act on His behalf and with His authority. **Similarly we are able to act in the name of Jesus and with His authority - on His behalf. This means that He initiates and we obey. We can exercise authority because we are under authority.**

This helps us to see that submission to the authority or Lordship of Jesus is an essential element of faith, both for those who need to be healed and those who exercise the authority to heal in the name of Jesus.

We see these principles being outworked in the succession of people who come with a humble spirit of submission to Jesus to be healed. In response Jesus spoke the word of healing.

For example, blind Bartimaeus cries out for Jesus to be merciful to him: *"Jesus, Son of David, have mercy on me!"*. He recognises he deserves nothing; his healing would be a work of God's mercy. When Jesus asks him, *"What do you want me to do for you?" (Mark 10: 51)* Bartimaeus asked for the return of his sight.

> *"Go," said Jesus, "your faith has healed you."*
> *Immediately he received his sight and followed Jesus*
> *along the road. (Mark 10: 52)*

Here again Jesus emphasised that the blind man's faith in Jesus had resulted in his healing. But Bartimaeus had not come with some dramatic profession of faith: "Oh Jesus, I believe, I really believe, I believe you will heal me," as so many do today! No, his faith was expressed in his expectation. He expected to receive his sight. He expected Jesus to heal him, which is why he would not allow anyone to deter him from crying out to Jesus.

It seems there can be a certain determination, desperation even, about faith. The Syro-Phoenician woman, a Gentile, was certainly desperate because her *"little daughter was possessed by an evil spirit" (Mark 7: 25)*. The woman found Jesus when He had gone to Tyre secretly and came and fell at His feet, begging Him to drive out the demon from her daughter.

Jesus was at first reluctant because His mission was foremost to the Jews. The woman persisted, *"Even the dogs under the table eat the children's crumbs" (Mark 7: 28)*. For such an answer, Jesus said that the woman could go, that the demon had left her daughter.

Again the humble approach to Jesus, the faith and the determination! This was also evident in the ruler whose daughter Jesus raised from the dead:

> *A ruler came and knelt before him and said, "My daughter has just died. But come and put your hand on her, and she will live." Jesus got up and went with him. (Matthew 9: 18-19)*

The centurion said that Jesus only needed to speak and his servant would be healed. He responded and spoke the word of healing. The ruler's faith is different. If Jesus lays His hands on his daughter, she will be healed. Again we see that Jesus responds exactly to the nature of the faith that is placed in Him. As He is on His way to the house a woman with another expression of faith presses through the crowd to touch Him.

> *She thought, "If I just touch his clothes, I will be healed." Immediately her bleeding stopped and she felt in her body that she was freed from her suffering. (Mark 5: 28-29)*

Jesus knew that power had gone out of Him because He had been touched by faith. The disciples were amazed that Jesus should ask who had touched Him as so many in the crowd were jostling Him. But He knew when He had been touched by faith. The woman fell at his feet - again the humble approach - and Jesus said to her:

> *Daughter, your faith has healed you. Go in peace and be freed from your suffering. (Mark 5: 34)*

Again the emphasis on faith! While this was taking place news arrived that the ruler's daughter had died.

> *Ignoring what they said, Jesus told the synagogue ruler, "Don't be afraid; just believe." (Mark 5: 36)*

The ruler had come to Jesus with the faith that his daughter would be healed if He came to her. Now Jesus encouraged him to persist in that faith, rather than believe the circumstances. **Faith in Jesus can change the circumstances!**

When Jesus came to the ruler's house, He put outside all who were lamenting the child's death, those who laughed at Him when He said that she was only 'sleeping'. In other words, He put the unbelief outside and only took the mother, father and the disciples with Him, into the room. He took the child by the hand and commanded: *"Little girl, I say to you get up.' Immediately the girl got up and walked around"* (Mark 5: 41-42).

Again the persistence of faith was rewarded; again Jesus simply spoke the word of authority; again the faith put in Him was rewarded.

We could consider many of the other healings recorded in the gospel. However, today we cannot relate to Jesus as He was then, walking about on planet earth, healing the sick and driving out demons and raising the dead. We have to relate to Him as He is now, the Lord who is reigning victoriously in heaven.

We can learn much from these examples of the principles that lay behind the healings that took place:

- All healing is a work of God's mercy; we deserve nothing from Him.

- People came with an attitude of humble submission to Jesus when they needed to be healed. They placed themselves *under* His authority.

- They came with faith, expecting to be healed and set free.

- Jesus made it clear that this faith was the reason for their healing, even though they expressed that faith in a variety of ways.

- There was a determination in those who came; they *expected* to receive.

- Jesus responded precisely to the nature of the faith placed in Him.

- He acted with the authority He had been given by the Father, often simply speaking only a few words to accomplish the healing. No wonder:

> *They ran throughout that whole region and carried*
> *the sick on mats wherever they heard he was. And wherever*

he went - into villages, towns or countryside - they placed
the sick in the marketplaces. They begged him to let them
touch even the edge of his cloak, and all who touched
him were healed. (Mark 6: 55-56)

Here again is that determination and desperation of faith that Jesus certainly honoured.

And *"Jesus Christ is the same yesterday and today and forever."* *(Hebrews 13: 8)* **He has lost none of His power to heal, His desire to heal, His willingness to heal those who come humbly to Him with faith in His mercy, expecting to receive from Him.**

4

JESUS HEALS TODAY: THROUGH HIS WORD

At first we might think that it would be wonderful if Jesus were available to us today as He was in the days of His earthly ministry. In truth He is more accessible to believers now than He was then. While on earth He could only be at one place at one time; now we have access to His throne of grace anywhere at anytime. Then a person had to gain access to Jesus; now every believer is given free access to come to Him whenever he or she chooses.

So we need to see how to take advantage of this access. How can we come to Jesus now and receive from Him? The scripture shows us three main ways: through God's Word, in prayer and through the ministry of His Church.

It is possible, easy even, to receive from God through His Word, in response to our prayers of faith and through the ministry of other believers. A key scripture to help us understand that the healing flow of God is contained in His words is found in Proverbs:

My son, pay attention to what I say; listen closely to my words.
Do not let them out of your sight, keep them within your heart;

for they are life to those who find them and health to a man's
whole body. (Proverbs 4: 20-22)

God's words contain His life, including *"health to a man's whole*
body". If we learn how to receive this life and health, they can
prevent us from becoming sick, as well as providing healing if we
are attacked by sickness. However, it is necessary for God's words
to be *transferred* from the Bible into our hearts, so that we believe
from the heart what He says.

God spoke and creation came into being. The Word that went
forth from His mouth was Jesus.

Through him all things were made; without him nothing
was made that has been made. In him was life, and that life
was the light of men. (John 1: 3-4)

It is not surprising, therefore, that when *"the Word became flesh and*
made his dwelling among us," (John 1: 14) that great things
happened when He spoke. No wonder the sick were healed, the
blind delivered and even the dead raised simply by Jesus speaking
a word of command or release: *"Get up and walk"* and the lame
were healed; *"Be opened"* and blind eyes were opened, the deaf
heard and the dumb spoke; *"Your faith has healed you"*, and God's
power brought release to the sick; *"Go"* and demons were cast out!

Jesus said that His words were *"spirit and life"*. They contain the life
of God's Spirit because they are the very words of God Himself.
This is as true of the words of the Old Testament as of the New.
Whether God spoke from heaven to the prophets, or on earth
through His Son, they are still the words of God Himself and

contain His life and power. Jesus was speaking from heaven long before He came to earth! Paul says:

> *For God, who said, "Let light shine out of darkness,"*
> *made his light shine in our hearts to give us the light of the*
> *knowledge of the glory of God in the face of Christ.*
> *(2 Corinthians 4: 6)*

Notice that God has taken the initiative and made His light to shine in the hearts of those who believe in Him, to give them the revelation of the truth. And He wants to reveal His glory in their lives. Paul explains that *"we have this treasure in jars of clay to show that this all-surpassing power is from God"* (2 Corinthians 4: 7). **This is the power in you as a believer in Jesus, and the Lord wants to see that power released, not only to meet every need in your life but also to flow out of you as rivers of life to others.**

… THE LORD WANTS TO SEE THAT POWER RELEASED, NOT ONLY TO MEET EVERY NEED IN YOUR LIFE, BUT ALSO TO FLOW OUT OF YOU AS RIVERS OF LIFE TO OTHERS.

The problem is that it is so easy to concentrate on the jar of clay instead of the treasure within, especially when that jar is in need of healing! Paul goes on to speak of an important principle:

> *It is written: "I believed; therefore I have spoken."*
> *With that same spirit of faith we also believe and*
> *therefore speak. (2 Corinthians 4: 13)*

Now if God's life and power is in His words, it does not matter who speaks them! The power is not in the mouth but in the words that the mouth speaks. And we can speak God's words of life and health over our lives. Jesus says that from the overflow of the heart the mouth speaks! It is not a matter of learning a faith formula and repeating this endlessly. The words we speak over our lives need to come from the heart.

There is little point in saying one thing when we pray and the very opposite when in conversation with others. Which do we truly believe? If there is faith in the heart there will be a consistency about what is said whether in prayer or conversation. The words spoken will be an expression of the thoughts of the heart.

BY BUILDING A DEPOSIT OF GOD'S WORDS IN OUR HEARTS WE ARE ABLE TO WALK IN HEALTH AND RESIST SICKNESS.

This is why the verses quoted from Proverbs are so important. It is wise to store the words of God's truth and life within us, so that when a need arises we already have the resources to meet that need. The *"shield of faith which is the Word of God"* is already in place. That shield is able to quench *"all the fiery darts of the evil one"*, including his desire to inflict sickness on people.

By building a deposit of God's words in our hearts we are able to walk in health and resist sickness. However, it was the sick who came to Jesus, and it was His words that healed them. So it must also be possible to take hold of His words and through them receive the spirit, life and healing that are contained in these words. There are a number of ways in which this can be done.

Words are to be spoken, and you can learn to speak God's words of healing over your own life and over the lives of others for whom you pray! Here is a simple way to do this.

First, receive the word. Remember, the words spoken need to come from the heart. So it is necessary to 'receive' the word into your heart: to receive the words of life, healing, power or whatever else is needed.

Let Jesus speak His words to you personally. God has supplied us with the scriptures as an amazing resource of those words of life. You can take any relevant scripture and let God speak this to you. Sit quietly and repeat the words of the verse of scripture you have chosen slowly a number of times, as if Jesus were speaking those words to you. As you do this, *believe* that the life and healing power of God contained in those words are being released in you.

BECAUSE JESUS HAS ALREADY ACCOMPLISHED YOUR HEALING THROUGH WHAT HE DID ON THE CROSS, THAT HEALING IS AVAILABLE TO YOU NOW

Faith has nothing to do with feelings, and so as you do this you may feel nothing is happening. Do not be deterred by this. Rarely will there be an immediate spectacular miracle. But you are not after the spectacular; you want to be healed! You do not have to wait for a spectacular event. **Because Jesus has already accomplished your healing through what He did on the cross, that healing is available to you NOW, and can be received NOW. If His words are life and health, you can take these words NOW and receive the life and health they contain NOW.**

I have used this method of receiving the life of God's Word in prayer for many years. I can praise God that He has kept me healthy and strong throughout that time. And I have known hundreds of people to receive their healing in this way.

Just as important is the fact that 'receiving' the word in this way builds faith that is effective when other methods of claiming God's healing grace are used. I have encouraged those who will receive the laying on of hands with prayer, to prepare for this event by 'receiving' the word in this way for a few days beforehand. Not only has the healing power been already initiated before we meet for prayer, but the person comes with a greater sense of expectation, for those words of healing have begun to live in his or her heart. It is possible to assent to something in the mind, but without such heart revelation.

... YOU CAN LIVE DAILY IN THE HEALING POWER OF JESUS AND RECEIVE FROM HIM THROUGH HIS WORD WITHOUT HAVING THE NEED OF ANYONE ELSE TO MINISTER HIS HEALING POWER TO YOU.

The point is this: **you can live daily in the healing power of Jesus and receive from Him through His Word without having the need of anyone else to minister His healing power to you.**

I speak much more extensively of this method of receiving from God through His words in my book, 'Listen and Live'. This contains a number of sections that will help you to receive from God through His Word. Here are a few of the scriptures you can use in particular relation to healing:

- I am the LORD who heals you.

- By my stripes you are healed.

- Peace I leave with you; my peace I give to you.

- He forgives all my sins and heals all my diseases.

- He sent forth his word and healed them.

- Your faith has healed you.

- He took up our infirmities and carried our diseases.

You can take these truths and 'personalise' them, so that the Lord is speaking directly to you. For example, instead of saying, "He sent forth his word and healed them", you can say: "I send forth my word and heal you". You can also add your name before or after the scripture: "I send forth my word and heal you, Colin."

Although you can use several scriptures, I suggest you use only one or two for a week. Repeat them for only three or four minutes at a time, for you will find it difficult to maintain concentration for longer periods. However, your attitude is important: that you regard this as three or four minutes of actually receiving God's healing life. Remember, you do not have to 'feel' anything, neither does a spectacular event have to take place. I have known people to be healed in this way from colds to cancer!

Once healed, continue to pray for a few minutes like this every day, and stay healthy. Prevention is better than cure!

When you pray in this or any other way, it is wise to first spend a few moments asking the Lord to forgive you for any sins and to ensure that you have forgiven any who have wronged you. You do not want anything to hinder your ability to receive from the Lord. Unforgiven sin and an unmerciful attitude towards others certainly have that effect.

5

SPEAKING TO THE MOUNTAINS

Not only is it possible to receive the life of God through His Word, but Jesus commands us to speak His truth to the situations of need in our lives. It is important to speak God's Word over your life and circumstances. It is also important to have an attitude of faith towards the problems and needs that arise in your life.

These needs cannot resist the power of God that you receive through His Word. His life is far greater than any need! Even though you may not have wonderful experiences at the time, yet you believe that every time you bring the life that is in the Word against the need in your life, in your body even, that need has to retreat before His power!

However, Jesus also tells us to speak to the mountains that arise: the needs that seem to block the way ahead for us. He said:

> *I tell you the truth, if you have faith and*
> *do not doubt, not only can you do what was done to*
> *the fig tree, but also you can say to this mountain,*

'Go, throw yourself into the sea,' and it will be done.
If you believe, you will receive whatever you ask in prayer.
(Matthew 21: 21-22)

Jesus had cursed the fig tree, and the disciples marvelled that it withered so quickly. This does not mean Jesus wants us to go around cursing things; but it demonstrates the authority with which He speaks. He uses this situation to teach the disciples that they too have such authority. They can command any mountain of need in their lives to move and be thrown *"into the sea"*, and it will be done! However, **Jesus makes clear that when they speak to the mountain, they must believe in their hearts and not doubt that it will be moved!**

JESUS MAKES CLEAR THAT WHEN THEY SPEAK TO THE MOUNTAIN, THEY MUST BELIEVE IN THEIR HEARTS AND NOT DOUBT THAT IT WILL BE MOVED!

This speaks to us of the true nature of faith. When you pray with true faith you *know* what the outcome of your prayer will be. You are not asking God to do something out of some vague hope that things will improve, nor do you believe that sometime in the future God will take notice of you, your need and your prayer.

As you receive through God's Word, you *know* His life is being imparted to you, whether you have any emotional experience or physical sensation, or not! And when you speak to the mountain of need you *know* in your heart that it has to be moved; it cannot stand against the authority with which you speak in the name of Jesus. There is certainly no point in speaking to a mountain with vague hope or unbelief!

When God spoke creation into being, He expected what He said would result in precisely what He had in mind. When Jesus spoke to mountains in people's lives, sicknesses were healed, demons fled and even the dead were raised. Many Christians fail to realise that speaking to mountains is, in God's eyes, an indispensable part of prayer. When Jesus taught the disciples to pray, He said:

> *"Have faith in God," Jesus answered. "I tell you the truth,*
> *if anyone says to this mountain, 'Go, throw yourself into the sea,'*
> *and does not doubt in his heart but believes that what he says*
> *will happen, it will be done for him. Therefore I tell you, whatever*
> *you ask for in prayer, believe that you have received it, and it will*
> *be yours. And when you stand praying, if you hold anything*
> *against anyone, forgive him, so that your Father in heaven*
> *may forgive you your sins." (Mark 11: 22-25)*

There are many important principles of prayer and faith mentioned in these few verses. It is possible to pray without first considering what we believe will happen as a result of our prayer!

1) Jesus says, *"Have faith in God."* This seems so self-evident, why did He say it? Your faith rests in your focus of concentration. It is possible to concentrate on yourself, your need, your sickness. When you do this, you spend your time in prayer talking or thinking about yourself and your problem, hoping that God is listening!

True prayer places the focus on God, on His love and almighty power, on what He has already accomplished for us on the cross. We can draw near to God:

Let us then approach the throne of grace with confidence,
so that we may receive mercy and find grace to help us
in our time of need. (Hebrews 4: 16)

When we pray, therefore, our focus is on the Lord, who sits on the throne of grace. He *"is able to make all grace abound to you"* (2 *Corinthians 9: 8).*

It is good to spend time worshipping Him, rather than your need! Praise Him for the victory He has already won that enables every need to be met in your life. Your faith is not in your sickness, so do not put your focus there. Neither is your faith in yourself, so do not focus on yourself. Your faith is not on your feelings, so do not focus on emotions. Your faith is not in an experience, so do not wait for one!

Your faith is in God, the One who is able to heal you, desires to heal you and has already provided for your healing. You see your need only through the eyes of what He has already accomplished!

2) Jesus then uses this phrase, *"I tell you the truth,"* meaning that even if you find this difficult to believe, nevertheless what follows is definitely, emphatically the truth!

3) *"If anyone says to this mountain..."* He speaks of anyone; that includes you. This is not authority reserved for a select few that appear to have a healing ministry. It is true for any believer!

4) The believer is to speak to the mountain. Yes, this is part of your prayer and an expression of your faith. It is doing precisely what Jesus Himself did, and what He commands you to do. Yes, this is a command, not a suggestion or a good idea.

Some wonder why their needs do not appear to have been met, yet they have never obeyed the command to speak to the mountain. We cannot complain if we do not see results when we do not act in the way Jesus commands!

5) This faith is expressed in speaking to the mountain, not thinking or talking about it! Again, this is where many believers miss the point. They do not sufficiently appreciate the authority Jesus has given them as believers.

> *I tell you the truth, whatever you bind on earth will*
> *be bound in heaven, and whatever you loose on earth*
> *will be loosed in heaven. (Matthew 18: 18)*

Jesus speaks of *"whatever"* - anything! To 'bind' means to prevent. You have the authority to prevent on earth whatever is prevented in heaven. To 'loose' is to release. So you have the authority to release on earth whatever is released from heaven!

If your 'mountain' does not exist in heaven, you have the authority to speak to it on earth and command that it be moved from your life. And you have the authority to release God's healing power into your life. Receiving that life through His Word is one way of doing this.

6) Jesus clearly says that when you speak to the mountain, you must believe that what you say will indeed happen. So He is not suggesting we use some faith formula without any relationship to

what we expect to happen. Anyone could say: "Mountain I command you to move in the name of Jesus." However such a command will only work if the one speaking it expects to be obeyed! Before speaking to your mountain, ask yourself what you *know* will happen as a result; not hope, but *know* will happen. This is true faith.

If you truly believe that the mountain of sickness *has* to move, then speak to it. However, sometimes you know that you do not have such expectations. What do you do in such a situation? There is no point in speaking to the mountain with doubt in your heart; Jesus makes this clear.

However, do not think that such faith is beyond you! You can do two things. First acknowledge your unbelief to the Lord and ask Him to forgive you, for unbelief is really a form of sin, of failing to trust in Him. He does not condemn you for this; He wants to forgive you and thus impart faith to you, for Jesus is the Author and Perfector of our faith!

Second, you can ask Him to cause faith to arise in your heart, that the Holy Spirit of truth will guide you into the truth of God's Word and inspire faith within you. Your perception of your situation changes immediately as the Holy Spirit 'speaks' God's Word to your heart. Whereas before you were filled with all kinds of uncertainty, now you know the truth of the matter because God has spoken to you by His Spirit.

7) Jesus says you are to speak to the mountain with faith, but does not say you are the one to actually move the sickness. No, this will be done for you.

God always honours the faith He inspires in you by His Holy Spirit and through His Word!

Nothing was impossible for Jesus; yet He never acted independently of His Father. He continually listened. As you listen to what He says in His Word, and as you 'receive' from Him, you will find that God works the faith in your heart. You somehow *know* the mountain has to be moved, that God has undertaken the matter *for* you. This may lead to a speedy result, or a more gradual process of healing. Nevertheless, you are certain of the outcome!

There is an important difference between listening to our emotions and listening to the Spirit. When emotions are involved in praying either for ourselves or those we love, it is very easy to be deceived unless we are careful.

We all know of situations where believers have said: "I really believe that God said He was going to heal him; then my friend died and my faith was shattered." What faith was shattered? Faith in a promise that had not come from God in the first place! How am I certain of this? For three reasons:

First, God always honours His promises. So it would not be possible for Him to give a promise He did not intend to keep!

Second, He knows the end from the beginning. From the eternal perspective, He can see the future as clearly as He can see the past. So He would not say that something was going to happen, if in fact He could see that it was not going to take place. He is not a man that He would lie!

Third, the Spirit guides us into the truth of what God *has said* in His Word, and especially of what He *has done* on the cross. When He speaks He points us to the accomplished work of Christ, for He knows this is what inspires true faith within us. Faith does not say that something is 'going to happen', but sees it as an already established reality.

> *Now faith is being sure of what we hope for and certain of what we do not see. (Hebrew 11: 1)*

Faith is being sure and certain. You see this certainty of faith in those who approached Jesus for healing. They came with certain expectation that they would receive their healing from Him, not some vague hope that something would happen at some time in the future.

Of course when we pray for those with whom we are involved emotionally, we *want* to believe that everything will be fine. It is easy, therefore, to listen to our own desires and imagine these are the words of the Spirit.

The test is always to judge what we 'hear' against the revelation of God's Word. Does He say He is going to heal, or that He has already done so by His stripes? Does this mean the Spirit will never give an indication of what is going to happen? No, but He will speak of definite action, not vague hope. Let me give you an illustration.

At a meeting I prayed with a man in a wheelchair. His pair of shoes was resting on his lap, so clearly he expected to walk home! I asked him if he always brought his shoes with him to a meeting. He replied that he had never done so before, although he had been prayed for on many occasions. However, God had told him to bring his shoes to the meeting that evening because he would be healed and would walk! He was healed and walked without any assistance.

This is an example of a specific word, spoken directly to the one with the need. This was not a vague promise given to a loved one.

Should we ignore this sense that God is going to heal someone? This is a difficult question to answer, for sometimes such a sense is unreal, does not come from God, and is merely the result of our own emotional desires. Yet, at other times, such thoughts can help us to maintain our persistence in prayer, either for ourselves or others. However, we still need to realise that the "I will" has to become "I have," for faith to operate genuinely in that particular situation.

8) Jesus then tells the disciples that no matter what they ask for in prayer, they are to believe they *have received* what they asked for. Not *will receive*, but *have received.*

This is truly the fruit of being sure and certain! **You *know* you have the answer. You *know* the outcome is assured. You *know* God has already undertaken in the matter, even if there is no apparent change in the circumstances immediately.** You cannot make yourself believe you have received it. This is an indication of arriving at that point of true faith, in which case you will thank the Lord for the outcome. Paul says:

> *Do not be anxious about anything, but in everything,*

*by prayer and petition, with thanksgiving, present your
requests to God. (Philippians 4: 6)*

The thanksgiving is so important, for how can we believe that we
have received what we ask for if we are not thankful? If someone
gives you a gift, you express your thanks, even though the gift may
be wrapped at that moment it is handed to you. When God 'gives'
us healing, it is sometimes like that. We *know* we have received,
even if there is no immediate manifestation of a miracle. We know
that the gift has been given and will be 'unwrapped'.

This is the outworking of what Jesus promises, *"Believe that you
have received it, and it will be yours."* It may be yours immediately,
or there may be a time delay. The healing may happen
spontaneously or over a period of time. **Yet you know you have
received the answer.** While waiting for the total manifestation of
the healing, you are no longer asking for the healing, but you are
thanking the Lord for what you believe you have received.

Let me beg you not to try to play games with God, nor to fool
yourself. Be completely honest with Him and yourself when you
doubt. He always responds to such honesty. He does not want to
withhold His blessings from you, neither is He making it difficult
for you to be healed. It is simply that He expects believers to
believe, and when **believers believe, believers receive!** He wants
you to trust in His grace, that He gives freely to those who deserve
nothing! We have already seen that such faith is implicit in
'receiving' the life and health that are in God's words. And we shall
see there are other ways in which we can receive what God has
chosen to give us through Jesus.

9) Finally, Jesus says that whenever we pray, we are not to *"... hold anything against anyone..."* rather, we are to forgive. Nothing else hinders your ability to hear from God more than unforgiveness. Every work of healing is a gift of God's mercy. We could never deserve to be healed. If God is to be merciful to us, we must be merciful to others.

Again this is a matter of the heart. If your heart is closed towards others, it becomes closed towards God. Whether we realise this or not, it is a spiritual truth. **Being merciful to others opens us up to receive mercy from the Lord.** Jesus said:

> *Blessed are the merciful, for they will be shown mercy.*
> *(Matthew 5: 7)*

What can you do if you do not 'feel' forgiveness towards someone? *Choose* to forgive him or her. Forgiveness is an act of the will; it is what you choose to do irrespective of your feelings. Often your feelings towards someone who has wronged you will not change until you have made the decision to forgive that person, and put the past behind you!

Does all this make praying for your healing a complicated matter? No, for to summarise, Jesus gives us clear instructions:

- Have faith in God.
- Speak to the mountain.
- Believe in your heart.
- Ask.
- Be thankful that you have received.
- Forgive any who have wronged you.

You can see that the element of faith is essential, and God's promises are sure!

> *Ask and it will be given to you ...*
> *For everyone who asks receives. (Luke 11: 9, 10)*

We can now see that Jesus teaches that we are to ask in faith; then we shall receive. The Greek here means literally: *"Go on asking and you will receive ... For everyone who continues to ask receives."*

If we pray with faith, why should we need to persist in asking? There are occasions when we do not truly believe when we first pray about a particular matter. Faith comes as we persist in asking, the Holy Spirit bringing the revelation of God's Word into our hearts.

You will sometimes experience this. You may have been praying for a situation for some time; then one day as you pray you suddenly realise: "That's it! It is done!" At that moment your prayer turns from asking to thanking. Now you will persevere in thanking until you see the full manifestation of what you asked God to do!

6

SPEAKING THE WORD

We have seen how to receive the spirit and life that is in God's Word. We have seen how Jesus teaches people to pray the prayer of faith, expressing the authority given to believers. When we speak to mountains of sickness or need, we are to believe in our hearts that those mountains will certainly be moved.

We have seen that Jesus has accomplished everything necessary for our healing through what He did on the cross. No matter what method of prayer or ministry is used, faith is to be at its heart.

Faith is a way of life, and cannot be reserved only for the times we pray or receive ministry! What we believe in between those times is of great importance, for God knows our thoughts at all times. We cannot convince Him of our faith when we pray while He has been listening to all our negative thoughts and fears, the product of unbelief rather than faith.

FAITH IS A WAY OF LIFE, AND CANNOT BE RESERVED ONLY FOR THE TIMES WE PRAY OR RECEIVE MINISTRY!

We therefore need to maintain our walk of faith at all times. Jesus warns us that from the overflow of the heart the mouth speaks.

And so our conversation is the real indication of what we believe in our hearts. This does not mean we are to learn a 'faith language', knowing the right things to say but not truly expressing what is in the heart. The faith needs to come from the heart.

TRUE FAITH RELEASES HIS GRACE INTO OUR CIRCUMSTANCES ...

We can hear what others say when praying with them; but we do not know what they are thinking and saying about their situation at other times! For during prayer times they know the right things to say! God is not going to heal because someone has discovered the right formula of words! Every healing is a work of His mercy and grace, not a reward for anything done by the Christian. **True faith releases His grace into our circumstances,** and true faith is what he believes in his heart!

When you believe, you 'see' the result. You are sure and certain of the outcome. You are not trying to make something happen by saying the right words. **You genuinely 'see' the healing with the spiritual eyes of faith. When this is the case, whatever you say about your circumstances is consistent with your 'seeing'.**

The natural man sees the sickness, speaks of the symptoms and believes the medical prognosis. **The man of faith sees the healing, speaks of God's goodness and grace, and believes what Jesus has accomplished for him. He 'sees' himself healed.** For him this is the reality of the situation and so it is only a matter of time before the symptoms disappear and the healing is fully manifested.

This is not a matter of someone saying he is healed when to everyone else there is clearly no such manifestation of healing.

There are some who try to do this, convinced that if they say that they are healed often enough, then eventually the healing must take place. God is not convinced by such tactics. **We do not confess we are healed in order to be healed, but because we believe we are healed. This is what we 'see'.**

Such 'seeing' enables you to receive from the Lord through His Word, or in any other way spoken of in scripture. You live in a constant flow of receiving rather than asking. Your prayer time is part of this whole process of healing, as is any time of ministry, through the laying on of hands, anointing or the agreement of faith with other believers.

In your heart there is a peace, a calm about the situation, an awareness that God is in complete control. Such a peace comes from believing what God has done for you on the cross and what He declares in His Word. It comes from believing that He is faithful to the promises He has given and will not deny your faith in the sacrifice of His Son.

This has a truly practical outworking in your life. **Your thinking, believing and speaking are all in line with the truth - and you speak accordingly, not only at prayer time, but all the time!**

YOUR THINKING, BELIEVING AND SPEAKING ARE ALL IN LINE WITH THE TRUTH - AND YOU SPEAK ACCORDINGLY, NOT ONLY AT PRAYER TIME, BUT ALL THE TIME!

You recognise that there is a difference between facts and truth. The fact is that you are sick; the truth is that by the stripes of Jesus you are healed. You 'see' that. It is revelation in your heart. The

... THE TRUTH HAS THE POWER TO CHANGE THE FACTS!

facts may be that you are manifesting certain symptoms. The truth is that Jesus bore your infirmities and carried your sicknesses when He went to the cross. The facts may suggest that nothing is happening when you pray, but your faith in the truth enables you to know that you are receiving your healing through God's grace.

Jesus is the Truth, and that Truth is eternal; nothing can undo what He has done or change what He has said. So the facts cannot alter the Truth; but **the Truth has the power to change the facts!**

The perseverance of faith in what you 'see' with your spiritual eyes enables you to continue to believe the Truth, even when there does not seem to be any change in the facts. The mistake made by many people is that they keep looking at the facts and doubt the truth! When they pray they are more aware of their symptoms than of the Lord, or His Word. When they receive ministry through the laying on of hands or anointing, they are disappointed if they do not have an immediate sensation of being healed, or a sudden removal of the symptoms. Their focus is on the facts rather than the Truth!

This is both understandable and natural. **But faith takes us beyond our understanding into the supernatural realities of God's truth, of what He has done for us in Jesus Christ.** The one who 'sees' with the eyes of faith keeps praising God for who He is and thanking Him for what He has done. The rest of His conversation is consistent with this.

Let me quote one example out of many. I prayed briefly at a meeting with a man who had a serious and painful back condition.

I spoke of these truths to him and the importance of maintaining his faith, irrespective of the circumstances. He later wrote to tell me that at the time I prayed with him, he felt nothing. There was no indication that healing had taken place. However, he put the teaching into practice and daily thanked the Lord for his healing because he had received it by faith.

Five days later he awoke to discover the condition had been totally healed, and all the pain and symptoms had disappeared. Interestingly, he told also of a friend who was prayed for at the same meeting with similar results. At the time of ministry he felt nothing, yet a few days later his healing was also completely manifested. Jesus promised:

... FAITH TAKES US BEYOND OUR UNDERSTANDING INTO THE SUPERNATURAL REALITIES OF GOD'S TRUTH ...

If you remain in me and my words remain in you, ask whatever you wish, and it will be given you. (John 15: 7)

Jesus does not say that there will always be immediate manifestation of what you ask for, but that *"it will be given you"*. This is the case because you remain in Him, you maintain your faith in Him. And His words remain in you, the spoken words of God. Through the teaching on faith, God had spoken to those two men. Those words remained in them - until their healings were manifested.

Does such a walk of faith mean that we will never doubt? No, but there is a difference between unbelief and doubt. Unbelief is an absence of faith. You may pray, but without faith, without expectation that you will surely receive from God. You may receive the laying on of hands, but go away thinking God did not heal unless there is an immediate manifestation of power and a removal of the symptoms.

Doubt, on the other hand is different. Basically you are in a position of faith, believing in God's faithfulness, knowing in your heart you have received from the Lord; yet there arise questions in your mind, or thoughts suggesting the outcome is doubtful. Such doubts are easily dealt with. Sometimes they are the product of what others have suggested, or they are a direct assault from the enemy. You ask the Lord to forgive the momentary doubts and immediately return to your faith position, praising God for the outcome.

All of us would prefer to receive instantaneous miracles that do not require a continual walk of faith! However, it is in such times of testing that our faith is both proved and strengthened. Only in this way can we learn to cling to the Lord in the face of adverse circumstances, not only concerning healing but other matters as well.

7

RECEIVING MINISTRY

The Church is to be the household of faith! Although each of us has a personal walk of faith with the Lord, we do so within the context of the Body of Christ to which, as believers, we belong. It is sad that there are many congregations where no opportunity for the healing ministry is given, especially when it is clear from scripture that every pastor and elder is to be involved in the ministry of healing. In the prophecy of Ezekiel, God spoke curse over the shepherds of Israel because they had failed to pastor His people properly:

> *You have not strengthened the weak or healed the sick or bound up the injured. (Ezekiel 34: 4)*

These are only some of His charges against them. The Lord promises that He will come and do the job properly: *"I will bind up the injured and strengthen the weak" (Ezekiel 34: 16)*. This prophecy was, of course, fulfilled in Jesus. All pastors and elders are to reflect His ministry, which is why Jesus says:

> *Is any one of you in trouble? He should pray. Is anyone happy? Let him sing songs of praise. Is any one of you sick?*

He should call the elders of the church to pray over him
and anoint him with oil in the name of the Lord.
And the prayer offered in faith will make the sick person well;
the Lord will raise him up. If he has sinned, he will be forgiven.
Therefore confess your sins to each other and pray for each
other so that you may be healed. The prayer of a righteous
man is powerful and effective. (James 5: 13-16)

There are several important truths to take hold of here:

- **The one who is in trouble should pray.** This, then, is the first reaction of a believer to any situation of need, including sickness. "He should pray." Of course he should pray with faith, believing he receives from the Lord.

- **If the matter is not resolved through his own prayer,** *"He should call the elders of the church to pray over him and anoint him with oil in the name of the Lord."* It is for the sick one to call the elders; it is not for the elders to offer to pray. Jesus waited for people to come to Him: the elders are to do likewise. The sick person is thereby acting in faith and obedience to God's Word.

- **The elders are those in spiritual leadership in the congregation and are expected to respond to the sick person's call upon them.**

- **These elders are to pray over the sick one with faith.** So they need to see themselves as channels of God's grace. His life and power will flow through this prayer to the believer.

- **These are words of scripture for all believers.** This instruction is directed to 'any' Christian who is sick - any believer in any congregation, for this letter is addressed to God's people scattered among the nations.

- **All elders should respond to such a call, and pray with faith for the sick.**

- **The elders are also to anoint with oil.** The healing is not in the oil, but in the Lord. In scripture God uses oil to anoint His people with His grace and power. It is a sign that God is imparting scriptural blessing to the one being anointed. Without faith this is simply a religious act. With faith it is a powerful means of God imparting His healing grace to His beloved children.

- **It is not the oil that will heal of itself, but the prayer of faith that accomplishes the anointing that will raise the sick one from his or her bed.**

- **Forgiveness is an important part of the healing process.** *Some* sickness is caused by sin, but all healing can be hindered by unforgiven sin. If a sickness is a direct consequence of sin, it can be easily healed once the cause is forgiven! Even though the condition may not be a direct result of sin, forgiveness of any and all sins opens up the way for the believer to receive his or her healing.

- **It is important that those administering the healing grace of God through prayer and anointing should also be free from all sins.** So they too are to confess their sins.

- **The scripture suggests that there will be open and mutual confession of sins.** Unless the elders are hiding sin, they should have nothing to fear from this. The picture given by Jesus is that of the elders joining the sick one in coming humbly before God, all being cleansed by Him; then the elders praying and anointing with oil, believing that through His grace, the believer will receive his or her healing.

- **The promise is:** *"The Lord will raise him up"*, not 'may', or 'might', or 'could'; but 'will'. When some suggest that they have been anointed but not raised up, the question remains as to whether these scriptural instructions as to what to do and believe were truly carried out!

- **The purpose of praying for one another is not to support each other in sickness, but** *"so that you may be healed"*. This is the expectation!

- *"The prayer of a righteous man is powerful and effective."* Of course when we confess our sins God not only forgives us but cleanses us from all unrighteousness! That restores us to the place of righteousness before God so that our prayer can be *"powerful and effective"*.

Such scriptures are a challenge to both faith and obedience, the two being very closely related! **God does not see His Church as a religious institution, but as a body of power-filled believers containing the ministry of His Kingdom here on earth.**

It hardly needs to be said that there is no mention in scripture of praying to Mary or any of the former saints, nor asking them to pray for us. The whole point of the cross is that God has opened up the way for us to have direct access to God Himself through Jesus Christ. He is the only intermediary between God and man. He has completed His work, making it possible to be at one with the Father and to receive directly from Him through the Holy Spirit.

Even the elders or other believers who pray for us are not to be thought of as intermediaries. They stand with the sick one in faith. **It is God who heals directly.** Acts such as the laying on of hands or anointing are 'points of contact' - actions that help the believer to receive directly from the Lord, what only He can give through His grace.

8

LAYING ON OF HANDS

Healing is not the prerogative of select individuals, but of every believer in the Lord Jesus Christ.

And these signs will accompany those who believe …
they will place their hands on sick people, and they will
get well. (Mark 16: 17, 18)

This promise is given within the context of disciples being sent out into the world to preach the good news of the Kingdom of God. Healing is one of the 'signs' that God gives to verify the authenticity of what we proclaim in His name. So in evangelistic situations, we should expect to see people healed, as they were both in the Gospels and the Acts of the Apostles. The gospel is the same today; so is the power of the Holy Spirit who enables our preaching!

When Jesus sent out the seventy-two, He told them to heal the sick and then proclaim the good news that this demonstrated the Kingdom of God was at hand!

However, healing is not confined to evangelistic situations. When preaching to the unsaved the faith of the believer is enough to see

IF OUR TRUST IS
IN THE LORD, THEN
THE METHOD HE USES
TO HEAL IS ONLY
OF SECONDARY
IMPORTANCE.

miracles of healing grace. God does not expect the unbelieving sinner to manifest faith. However, in the case of believers, God does expect faith both in those praying and those receiving the laying on of hands.

Often when healing in Jesus' name, speaking the word of healing with authority is enough. You do not necessarily have to lay hands on someone to whom you are witnessing. Often in public services, believers are healed through the word of authority spoken and received with faith! At others times it is appropriate for there to be ministry through laying on of hands.

It must be understood that this is not a magical cure-all, whereby people are automatically healed, simply because someone has laid hands on a person using the name of Jesus. It is a common occurrence for a minister of the gospel to pray for a number of people at a meeting. Some are healed, and some are not. Why? The same person, with the same faith and the same anointing has prayed for each! Is it that God wants to heal some and not others? No, for we have seen that He has made provision for all our healing needs. Clearly, then, some are in the place of faith to receive because their trust is in the Lord, not in the laying of hands.

There is a subtle truth here that we must grasp. **If our trust is in the Lord, then the method He uses to heal is only of secondary importance.** It does not matter whether it is through a word of authority, through being anointed by the elders, or receiving the laying on of hands in a service at a home prayer meeting or simply from Christian friends. These are only the various channels that the Lord uses to impart healing. Their faith is in Him, not in an action, an event or a moment of time. Each of these actions is an opportunity to express faith in *Him*.

There is not disappointment, therefore, if the laying on of hands is not accompanied by some dramatic event or wonderful experience. The goodness of God is being appropriated by faith!

If there is an immediate, dramatic or quiet manifestation, well and good. If, however, there is no apparent, immediate change this does not shake our faith in Jesus, for we believe we have received and go on our way thankful for His faithfulness to His words of promise.

The fact that some who have received go away disappointed is an indication that their faith was more in an event than in the Lord Himself. Where there is faith in the Lord there may be an immediate manifestation of healing. On the other hand, a healing process can take place in the believer in stages. He may receive the laying on of hands on a number of occasions and receive further healing each time, as he or she continues to look to the Lord for the complete manifestation of healing that is needed.

Jesus warns that we shall not be heard for our many words. **The authority with which those who pray with the laying on of hands is a significant factor, especially when mountains need to be moved and the demonic powers of infirmity need to be bound.** Faith and authority belong together!

In the final analysis faith is a very simple matter. It is unbelief that complicates the situation! In simplicity of faith children can lay hands on one another, and even on their parents, and see healing result. The children at Kingdom Faith are taught to expect to be used of God in this way as a normal part of their Christian lives and experience! Wonderful miracles often result!

Sometimes Christians are too quick to pray, without first pausing to consider what they expect to happen in response to the prayer! This is why results can be so unpredictable, a situation that does not glorify the Lord. And it is not encouraging for someone to receive prayer and ministry again and again and still not receive his or her healing. It is not helpful to others to see the same people go forward for ministry again and again and see them return to their places disappointed again and again.

It has to be said that this is because sometimes people receive the laying on of hands when this is not appropriate, especially when a crowd of people are receiving ministry within a few minutes. In such situations there is no time to inquire as to the faith of all those receiving prayer or of what their expectations are!

In pastoral situations, however, people can prepare their hearts before receiving ministry. I find it helpful to give people a few days to prepare, especially if a longstanding need is to be addressed. It is good that the person approaches the time of ministry with repentance and in faith.

The believer is bringing himself or herself to the Lord, trusting Him. **It is not the sickness that is being healed, but the believer is being healed from the sickness.** God does not want to deal with symptoms but to heal His child of all that has led to these symptoms being manifested. He wants to do a total work of healing on that person.

I have known many people to be concerned about a specific need, only for the Lord to show that He wants to do a far more thorough and complete work of healing. **His concern is for the whole person - spirit, soul and body.** We are to cast *all* our cares on Him, not try to live with some while asking him to heal others.

I have often found that the healing need that concerns the individual is not really the issue the Lord wants to address in his or her life. It is only a symptom of something far more significant. In addressing that deeper issue the more superficial needs are also met.

Here we have to be careful, for it is entirely detrimental to faith to take our eyes off the Lord and place them on ourselves by playing 'hunt the problem'. This is the mistake made by many Christians and even those trying to help them. Together they play 'hunt the problem' and immediately faith begins to evaporate.

Such deeper needs will come to light through revelation from God, not self-analysis. The Holy Spirit will show if there is a deeper need which has to be addressed and will give revelation of the nature of that need. As we are to pray *at all times* in the Spirit, we should always be listening to Him so we can pray for the issues He tells us to address.

There have been countless occasions when someone has asked me to pray for a specific issue. As I have begun to pray, the Holy Spirit has shown me that this is not the issue; that He wants to do a more far-reaching work in that person. He or she goes away with a much greater miracle that the one being sought: that is indeed the mercy of God!

Believers *"... will lay hands on the sick, and they will get well"*. The healing, of course, is God's work, not ours! **He is the Healer! Our part is to obey the Lord, following the leading of the Holy Spirit, knowing He will honour our faith and obedience.** And He is the One who never fails us when our trust is in Him!

9

'HEALERS'

We have already noted that we need to beware of occult 'healers' who claim to have a healing gift. There is no question that the devil who causes sickness can also remove it; but he leaves people in spiritual bondage in the process.

There was an occasion when two of the most noted occult healers in the country came to see me. They had seen many 'miracles' through calling on spirits to heal people. In the process they had themselves come into bondage to the demonic forces they had invoked for these 'healings'. They repented of their occult involvement, turned to Christ and were completely delivered from the demonic forces. Remember, the devil can appear as an 'angel of light'!

However, in one of the lists of ministries that operate in the Church through the Holy Spirit, Paul lists 'gifts of healings'. Now, this is often mistranslated as 'gift of healing' or 'gift of healings'. In the text both words are plural, 'gifts of healings'. To mis-translate the original can give the impression that to some are given a gift of healing. The correct translation, however, shows us that the gift is not in any individual, but in the healings that are given to those who are sick.

Clearly, some are given a healing ministry by God. There are those who are used regularly by God to impart His healing to others. Every believer can be used by God; those with healing ministries are used regularly by Him because He enables them to encourage and release faith in others to trust God for their healing. They become instruments of God's healing grace to others; but the healing belongs to the Lord Himself and so *all* the glory belongs to Him for those things that take place.

Many aspire to have healing ministries; they want to be used by God in this particular way. The first requirement of such a ministry is compassion for the sick, as with Jesus. Together with this compassion will be faith and the ability to exercise authority over sickness, commanding people to be released in the name of Jesus.

How can you identify those who have such ministries? By their results - or 'fruit" to use Jesus' word! It is not what a person claims, but what can clearly be seen to be the fruit of his or her ministry.

Healing in the name of Jesus will not lead to any harmful spiritual side-effects as with occult healing, but will rather enhance the spiritual life of the one who is healed. Neither will there be any harmful effects on the one being used by God. He or she will humbly give thanks to God for the privilege of being used for His glory manifested in the healing of His people!

10

HOLY COMMUNION

Holy Communion, the Lord's Supper, or the Eucharist, is a wonderful means given by Jesus to enable His people to receive healing in their lives. Many who receive this sacrament of God's grace regularly, do not understand how this can be a means of God's healing in their lives. This is not a new problem; it was the case also in New Testament times. Paul said:

> *For anyone who eats and drinks without recognising*
> *the body of the Lord eats and drinks judgement on himself.*
> *That is why many among you are weak and sick, and a number*
> *of you have fallen asleep. (1 Corinthians 11: 29-30)*

By 'fallen asleep' Paul means died! Many are weak and sick and some have died because they have not recognised the body of the Lord. What does the apostle mean?

When Jesus took the bread He said, *"This is my body".* When He took the cup, He said, *"This is my blood of the new covenant".* **When Jesus sacrificed His body on the cross and shed His blood for us, He accomplished all that was necessary for our forgiveness, salvation and healing of spirit, soul and body.**

Whenever we celebrate the Lord's Supper we *"... proclaim the Lord's death until he comes". (1 Corinthians 11: 26)* This is not a memorial, but a proclamation! **It is a proclamation that all that Jesus died to give us is indeed ours NOW through His grace and mercy, everything that is needed for our bodily sustenance, strength and healing, as well as everything necessary for our forgiveness and healing.**

As with the word of authority, anointing or the laying on of hands, so Holy Communion can be a channel of God's healing grace to us as, by faith, we lay hold of all that He accomplished for us on the cross. Paul seems to say that some were approaching the Lord's Supper with a casual attitude, without such faith to lay hold of the finished work of the cross. As a result many were weak and sick and some had experienced a premature death.

This is not an invitation to stand in judgement on anyone else, but rather an encouragement to our own faith, to see what a wonderful means of God's healing grace this is. More than that, regular receiving of this sacrament with faith can keep our bodies fit and strong, and our lives cleansed of sin. In Jesus' body is all that is needed for our bodily strength, health and sustenance.

Again it is a matter of what you believe. If you treat Communion simply as a memorial of a past event, then it will not have this dynamic effect on your life! If, however, you believe that you receive afresh the virtue of Christ's body and blood, you will indeed be blessed by a fresh impartation and release of His life in your life.

This does not mean you have to believe that the bread becomes the physical body or the wine His physical blood. But it does mean that you believe you are able to appropriate all the benefits of both His body and blood as you receive from Him by faith!

POSTSCRIPT

So much has been left unsaid in such a short book. There is sufficient encouragement to your faith to see that God is able to heal you and desires to do so. You can live every day of your life in His healing grace. He gave His life for your salvation, your complete healing of spirit, soul and body.

If you have not already done so, begin to put the teaching of this book into practice. Turn to the Gospels and the whole of the New Testament with a different mindset, knowing God wants to speak to you personally, meet with you personally and pour His healing grace into your life personally.

Do not think that the instantaneous miracle is the only way in which God heals. There is healing in His Word, in His Spirit who lives within you as a believer. He can heal directly through His Word, through a word spoken with authority by you or others so that mountains of sickness are moved in the name of Jesus. He can further His healing work in you through anointing, the laying on of hands, through receiving Holy Communion. **Healing is so much a part of God's purpose, He has provided so many different ways of receiving His healing grace!**

And know that He can use you to be an instrument of healing grace in the lives of other people. You can learn to speak to mountains of need in others' lives and see them moved. You can lay hands on the sick and see them recover.

If at first the results seem disappointing, do not be deterred. Persevere, seeking to depend on the Holy Spirit to lead you and work through you. And every work of healing will give glory and honour to the Father and the Son, through the Holy Spirit's activity in and through you. To Him belongs all the praise!

FURTHER READING

For a more indepth look at the teaching of scripture on healing read Colin Urquhart's book:

God's Plan For Your Healing, published by Marshall Pickering.

Other related books by Colin Urquhart:

True Prayer - What it means to pray in the name of Jesus.
Listen and Live - How to receive from the Lord through His Word.
Anything you Ask - How to pray with faith and see your prayers answered!
The Truth that Sets you Free - a 'must' for all those involved in ministering to others.

CASSETTE SERIES RELATED TO HEALING:

Healing - A set of 12 messages (6 tapes) on healing.
Healing & Deliverance - A set of 3 messages.
Healing Grace - A set of 3 messages.

All the above are available from Kingdom Faith Resources
(see details below).

The True Series currently comprises the following titles:

TRUE AUTHORITY
TRUE CHURCH
TRUE COVENANT
TRUE DISCIPLES
TRUE FAITH
TRUE GOD
TRUE GRACE
TRUE HEALING
TRUE LIFE
TRUE LOVE
TRUE PRAYER
TRUE SALVATION
TRUE SPIRIT
TRUE WORSHIP

All these books by Colin Urquhart and a catalogue of other titles and teaching materials can be obtained from:

Kingdom Faith Resources, Roffey Place, Old Crawley Road
Faygate, Horsham, West Sussex RH12 4RU.
Telephone 01293 854 600 email: resources@kingdomfaith.com